AIRCRAFT

Fire-Fighting Aircraft and Smoke Jumpers

Henry M. Holden

Enslow Publishers, Inc.

40 Industrial Road	PO Box 38
Box 398	Aldershot
Berkeley Heights, NJ 07922	Hants GU12 6BP
USA	UK

http://www.enslow.com

Library of Congress Cataloging-in-Publication Data

Holden, Henry M.
    Fire-fighting aircraft and smoke jumpers / Henry M. Holden.
       p. cm. — (Aircraft)
    Includes bibliographical references and index.
    Summary: Presents firsthand pilot accounts and examines pilot training, aircraft specifications, and specialized equipment used in fighting wildfires from the air.
    ISBN 0-7660-1720-6
       1. Aeronautics in forest fire control—United States—Juvenile literature.
    2. Smokejumpers—United States—Juvenile literature. [1. Smokejumpers.
    2. Wildfire fighters. 3. Fire fighters.] I. Title. II. Aircraft (Berkeley Heights, N.J.)
    SD421.43 .H65 2002
    634.9'618—dc21

                            2001007055

Printed in the United States of America

10 9 8 7 6 5 4 3 2 1

To Our Readers: We have done our best to make sure all Internet Addresses in this book were active and appropriate when we went to press. However, the author and the publisher have no control over and assume no liability for the material available on those Internet sites or on other Web sites they may link to. Any comments or suggestions can be sent by e-mail to comments@enslow.com or to the address on the back cover.

Photo Credits: Bombardier Aerospace, Amphibious Aircraft, pp. 1, 4–5, 13, 15(T); Bureau of Land Management, pp. 8, 12, 14(T), 18, 20, 21, 23(T), 28, 32, 34, 40, 42; © Corel Corporation, pp. 3, 11, 24, 30, 35; Department of Defense, p. 16; Henry M. Holden, pp. 7, 22(T), 36, 38; Lockheed Martin Corporation, p. 15(B); NASA, pp. 17, 26; Sikorsky Helicopters/United Technologies, Inc., pp. 19, 23(B); U.S. Navy, pp. 14(B), 22(B).

Cover Photo: Bombardier Aerospace, Amphibious Aircraft.

Contents

CHAPTER 1

Wildfire

The storm started at 1:23 A.M. in late August 1999. Over the next five hours, more than 3,000 lightning flashes lit up the dark sky of Redding, California. Some of the lightning strikes started brush fires. Others hit trees, igniting them like matches.

Lightning is so hot that the sap within a stricken tree boils.

One lightning bolt hit a tall pine tree. The lightning traveled down the inside, into the roots. The roots began to heat like barbecue coals. Suddenly there was a flash. The fire ignited the pine needles on the ground, and the flames quickly traveled up the tree. The wind blew the sparks to the next tree, and then to several more trees. The trees exploded into flames.

Forest fires can spread quickly. Along the windy tops of the trees, they can travel at twenty miles per hour. They travel more slowly near the ground.

Sizing Up the Fire

At dawn, forest ranger Vickie Lamoureux stood in the lookout tower atop the 2,600-foot Bear Mountain, more than 30 miles away. She could see dozens of thick smoke columns rising from the green forest. She knew there could be homes and people in danger. Lamoureux picked up her radio and called the fire control center (FCC). The FCC would find out the size of the fire and the direction in which it was traveling. To do this, they would call for an airplane to fly over the fire.[1] This aircraft is called the lead plane.

A lead plane is fast and highly maneuverable. It may be a small single- or twin-engine airplane such as a King Air C90B. The King Air is a turboprop that uses jet engines to turn the propellers. As the lead plane, it carries one or two pilots.

Specifications for
Beechcraft King Air C90B

Height—14 feet 3 inches
Length—35 feet 6 inches
Wingspan—50 feet 3 inches
Engines—2
Crew—1 or 2
Cruise speed—275 miles per hour

The lead plane flew over the fire area. The pilot saw that the fire was growing larger. To the east, a cluster of retirement homes and a Boy Scout camp were in danger. The town of Shingletown was to the north, and the village of Manton was to the south. Disaster loomed in different directions. The pilot radioed back to the FCC and reported the direction and speed of the fire. People in the

Single-engine lead planes are used to survey the size and direction of wildfires. This lead plane is the Beechcraft T-34 Mentor, an ex-military training aircraft.

path of the fire would be warned to leave their homes. When wildfires get out of control, they can quickly destroy homes and kill animals and people.

By late afternoon, more than five hundred acres of forest were on fire. It was time to launch an air strike.[2]

Flying Fire Trucks

An air strike is a combination of aerial tankers and helicopters. These aircraft drop fire retardant, foam, or water on the fire. Aerial tankers are like flying fire trucks. They are usually modified military bombers or propeller-driven cargo planes and airliners. A tanker will swoop in and follow the lead plane over the fiery landscape to the drop point, about 150 feet above the treetops. It will splash fire retardant around the fire. If the fire is starved of new fuel, such as other trees and brush, it will go out. A second tanker will follow, a few hundred feet behind.

"We try to keep the fixed wings on one side of the fire, the helicopters on the other, and bring them in one at a time," said Bill Buckley, a lead plane pilot.[3] This way the planes and helicopters will not crash into each other.

To help combat the California fire, two Grumman S-2T Tracker air tankers flew through the smoke-filled canyons. Their mission was to drop fire retardant between the wildfire and the threatened residences it was moving toward. With red-hot cinders flying all around them, the pilots were depending on both their piloting skills and fire-fighting aircraft to complete this task. After a successful drop, the fire was surrounded with the retardant.

The air tankers headed back to the base to fill up with another load of retardant. A lone helicopter was sent into the danger zone to drop water directly onto the flames. Unfortunately, this did not extinguish the fire. The fire was doused in certain areas, but it kept growing larger and gaining ground in others. Eventually, the wildfire made its way past the retardant line.

The Next Step

The aerial attack alone had not been able to control the forest fire. Ground troops were called in to build a fire line in front of the approaching flames. Using hoses, chainsaws, axes, shovels, bulldozers, and fire engines, the individuals on the ground cut down the plants and shrubs next to the fire. They hoped to cut off the path of the fire before it reached Shingletown, Manton, or any other surrounding neighborhoods.

As night approached, the darkness and a layer of smoke in the sky prevented any further aerial attack. Working by the light from lanterns on their helmets, ground firefighters continued the assault on the wildfire. Stumbling over the rocky terrain and warding off mosquitoes, the men and women on the ground did their best to stop the approaching flames.

With only an occasional break, they continued to remove all flammable materials—brush, fallen trees, and roots—from the fire's path for the next few days. Aerial fire fighting resumed during the day, and the menacing flames were eventually extinguished.

A large fire can keep air tankers and firefighters working nonstop for several days. It took three days to put this California fire out. It burned seven hundred acres of timberland and left nothing but the skinny, charred skeletons of trees rising from a carpet of gray ash. Luckily, with the quick actions of aerial and ground firefighters, many lives and homes had been saved.

CHAPTER 2

Flying on the Edge of Danger

Fighting wildfires from the air is one of the most dangerous jobs a pilot can do. Air tanker pilots fly very low over mountains and rugged ground. Heat rising from the fire creates turbulence, and shifting winds can make flying over the smoke and fire even more dangerous. The thick smoke can hide electric power lines in the canyons.

Sometimes the air tankers fly in alone, but it is safer to use a lead plane. "This airplane carries the air attack supervisor. He is like an airborne air traffic controller," said Jean Bergerson of the Fire Control Center in Grand Rapids, Michigan. "He determines what altitudes and areas the aircraft involved will fly." Sometimes as many as twenty-four aircraft fly in an area of only a few square miles. "It is important for someone to keep track of all of them in order to maintain a safe operation," said Bergerson.[1]

When fighting large fires, air tanker pilots will take off and land several times a day. This is very tiring and can lead to accidents. For example, on the night of August 28, 2001, two pilots died when their air tankers collided over a raging two-hundred-acre fire in Mendocino County, California.[2]

≡ *Fire-Fighting Aircraft*

Many different propeller-driven aircraft fight wildfires. An air strike may involve a fifty-year-old Douglas DC-6B. At one time, this airplane carried about one hundred passengers in comfort. Now it carries a tank filled with 3,000 gallons of fire retardant chemicals. This airplane has four powerful 2,500-horsepower engines. (By comparison, a car engine has 150 to 200 horsepower.)

The Douglas DC-6B is one type of air tanker used to help put out a wildfire. Here, it is dropping about 3,000 gallons of fire retardant.

The Canadair CL-415 is actually a flying boat with probes in its belly to help scoop up water.

The Grumman S-2T Tracker is a former military aircraft. It has a 1,200-gallon tank inside. It is another aerial tanker used to fight forest fires.

Another air tanker specifically designed to fight wildfires is the Canadair CL-415, called the Super Scooper. It can fly down to a lake and scoop water into its belly. Twelve seconds later, the plane can fly off with 1,600 gallons of water in its tanks. Its four-door tank system can hold water or a foam mixture.

The Lockheed C-130 Hercules can also help combat wildfires. As an air tanker, it is equipped with fire retardant chemical tanks called the Modular Airborne Fire-Fighting System (MAFFS). By using MAFFS, the flow

Douglas DC-6B

Height—28 feet 5 inches

Length—105 feet 7 inches

Wingspan—117 feet 6 inches

Engines—4

Crew—3

Cruise speed—308 miles per hour

Tank capacity—3,000 gallons

Douglas DC-6B

Grumman S-2T Tracker

Height—16 feet 3 inches

Length—43 feet 6 inches

Wingspan—72 feet 7 inches

Engines—2

Crew—1 or 2

Cruise speed—242 miles per hour

Grumman S-2T Tracker

Tank capacity—1,200 gallons

Canadair CL-415

Height—29 feet 6 inches

Length—65 feet

Wingspan—93 feet 8 inches

Engines—2

Crew—2

Cruise speed—233 miles per hour

Tank capacity—1,600 gallons

Canadair CL-415

Lockheed C-130 Hercules

Height—38 feet 3 inches

Length—97 feet 9 inches

Wingspan—132 feet 7 inches

Engines—4

Crew—3

Cruise speed—345 miles per hour

Lockheed C-130 Hercules

Tank capacity—3,000 gallons

This four-engine Lockheed C-130 Hercules can carry up to 3,000 gallons of water, foam, or fire retardant.

rate for a retardant drop over a fire can be preselected depending on the intensity of the wildfire. At maximum flow rate, a MAFFS-equipped Lockheed C-130 Hercules can release its entire contents in less than five seconds.

Large numerals on each airplane help the lead plane pilot tell the aircraft apart. Many have bright orange markings so that other air tanker pilots can see them.

≡ Choppers on the Job

Helicopters are another form of flying fire truck. They can carry hundreds of gallons of water to a wildfire. Using either buckets called Bambi Buckets or external tanks attached to the helicopter, the chopper becomes a water bomber. The Bambi Bucket was named for the Disney deer that lost his mother in a forest fire.

To fill a Bambi Bucket, the pilot hovers over a nearby lake or other water source and lowers the bucket into the water. A strong steel cable holds the bucket. The helicopter hauls up the filled bucket and flies over a flaming area. The pilot then pulls a release trigger that opens the bottom of the bucket, releasing the water on the flames.

The helicopter can slow down and, if necessary, hover over the fire. This means it can drop water on the fire with great accuracy. At the last minute, the pilot can change the drop point if the fire changes direction.

Using helicopters for water drops, or helitack missions, has a special advantage over using fixed-wing air tankers in fighting wildfires. Helicopters can fly low and close to the fire. As a general rule, they usually start their water drop about fifty feet above the fire.[3]

This Bell UH-1 Huey helicopter is scooping water from a lake into its Bambi Bucket.

Helicopter pilots have to be very careful not to make sudden moves with the helicopter when transporting water in a bucket. The bucket, hanging below the chopper, can start to swing back and forth. The bucket could pull the pilot in a direction in which he does not want to go. If the pilot is not careful, the bucket could pull the chopper into the fire, or the pilot could lose control and crash.

Former military helicopters such as the Bell UH-1 Huey or the Bell AH-1 Cobra may carry three hundred to six hundred gallons of water in their Bambi Buckets. Large helicopters such as the Sikorsky S-64 Skycrane can carry between one thousand and three thousand gallons of

Transporting water in a bucket to the scene of a wildfire can be a very dangerous mission for helicopter pilots. This helicopter is the Sikorsky S-64 Skycrane.

The Sikorsky S-70 Firehawk can carry up to fifteen firefighters to a fire zone or drop one thousand gallons of water on a wildfire.

water or retardant. Most of the time, they dip a Bambi Bucket into a nearby lake and carry the load underneath the helicopter. Some helicopters, such as the Sikorsky S-70 Firehawk, can draw one thousand gallons of water from a lake through a snorkel into a tank attached to its fuselage.

Helicopters can also carry firefighters to a fire. If the desired landing area is too small for a landing, the firefighters will slide down ropes. Once the ground firefighters set up base camps, helicopters can carry in supplies. If the firefighters become injured or made sick by the smoke, helicopters are used to rescue them. Pilots call this a short-haul rescue.

A short-haul rescue is an emergency rescue method to quickly get a person out of a dangerous situation. This

A short-haul rescue can be dangerous. The rescuer has to first stand on the helicopter skid, and then lower himself on a cable from a helicopter to the injured person below.

type of rescue is very risky. A cable suspended from a hovering chopper lowers a rescuer to the victim below. Usually the rescuer rigs a harness to the victim. If the injuries are serious, the victim is placed in a stretcher. The helicopter then lifts both the victim and the rescuer, suspended from the cable, to safety a short distance away. Crews do short-haul rescues only when there is good visibility.[4]

The Dangers of Flying

The heat from a wildfire can sometimes cause one or more of an airplane's engines to fail. Jim Cook has been flying tankers for twenty-three years. "Five times [my plane] has been on fire, and [I] had to make thirty-eight landings with one engine out," he said.[5]

The smoke can rob the engines of the fresh air they need to operate. It can cause the engines to lose power. A loss of power may mean the airplane will not be able to continue to fly. If the engine stops, it cannot always be

Smoke from a wildfire can create many risky flying conditions for pilots.

restarted. This is one reason pilots never like to drop retardant up mountainsides. If they have a mechanical problem such as an engine failure, they could crash into the mountain.[6] At only 150 feet above the treetops, the pilot will not have time to land safely.

Large wildfires make flying very challenging for a pilot. These wildfires create their own weather conditions. The clouds of smoke can travel up to 30,000 feet high. They can form a dome over the fire and hold the heat in. It is dangerous to fly underneath this smoky dome. It can be like flying into a furnace.[7]

Wildfires draw oxygen from the surrounding air. This creates wind. Sometimes these winds can exceed the force of a hurricane. The rising flames create superheated winds. These winds can travel thousands of feet high and mix with the cooler air at high altitudes. This creates more wind and more fires.

Bell AH-1 Cobra

Height—14 feet
6 inches

Length—53 feet 1 inch

**Main rotor
diameter**—44 feet
10 inches

Engine—1

Crew—1 or 2

Cruise speed—about 140 miles per hour

External 300-gallon Bambi Bucket

Bell AH-1 Cobra

Bell UH-1 Huey

Height—12 feet
10 inches

Length—57 feet
3 inches

**Main rotor
diameter**—44 feet

Engine—2

Crew—2

Cruise speed—115 miles per hour

External 300-gallon Bambi Bucket

Bell UH-1 Huey

Sikorsky S-64 Skycrane

Height—25 feet 5 inches
Length—88 feet
Main rotor diameter—72 feet 1 inch
Engine—2
Crew—2
Cruise speed—126 miles per hour
External 3,000-gallon Bambi Bucket

Sikorsky S-64 Skycrane

Sikorsky S-70 Firehawk

Height—16 feet 9 inches
Length—64 feet 10 inches
Main rotor diameter—53 feet 8 inches
Engines—2
Crew—2
Cruise speed—171 miles per hour
Tank capacity (internal)—1,000 gallons

Sikorsky S-70 Firehawk

CHAPTER 3

Fire-Fighting Equipment

Fighting wildfires requires many pieces of equipment. High-tech electronics on airplanes, such as infrared sensors, can see through smoke. Satellites and laptop computers are used to monitor the fire and to help keep track of firefighters on the ground.

Some fire-fighting aircraft use the Global Positioning System (GPS) to navigate to the exact location of the fire. The GPS uses signals from some of the 24 GPS satellites orbiting 12,500 miles above Earth. The GPS records the aircraft's speed and location. It feeds this information into a computer in the air tanker. The computer also contains the exact location of the fire and plots the shortest route to it. On some large air tankers, the computer controls the tanker doors under the plane. The computer opens the doors and automatically adjusts the flow of retardant at just the right point over the fire. The computer can adjust the flow depending on the fire's intensity.

During the summer, wildfires usually break out in several forests at the same time. The U.S. Forest Service uses satellite data from the National Aeronautics and Space Administration (NASA) to locate wildfires. NASA's *Terra* satellite orbits more than five hundred miles out in space. It can provide a view of fires across the entire United States. It transmits daily images of wildfires to the U.S. Forest Service within minutes of the time that the satellite passes over the region. This helps the Forest Service to get a big picture of all the fires and to manage its resources effectively.[1]

≡ Sensors to the Rescue

Sometimes the smoke from a wildfire is so thick that the flames cannot be seen from the air. This is where forward-looking infrared (FLIR) sensors help. The heat-sensitive eye of an FLIR system is in a camera mounted beneath the airplane or helicopter. Someone inside the aircraft can move this eye. An onboard monitor shows cold objects as dark gray or black. Hot objects appear light gray or white. The FLIR can detect the heat through clouds and smoke and can even help the operator see at night. A zoom lens helps to close in and tell humans from animals. Some

NASA scientists from the Kennedy Space Center are flying in a Be
UH-1 Huey helicopter over a wildfire in Florida. They are using FLI
and a small monitor to see the path of the fire.

infrared equipment can detect a sixteen-inch-wide hot
spot from eight thousand feet.[2] Even if the smoke hides
the firefighters on the ground, the FLIR can detect their
body heat. This is helpful because, if the flames are
surrounding the firefighters, the FLIR operator can radio
the firefighters to help them escape.

Fighting Fire with Fire

Firefighters sometimes set a fire to put another fire out.
They call this second fire a backfire. A backfire is set in
front of the first wildfire and burns the brush in its path.
Strong winds from the oncoming fire pull the flames

of the backfire toward the big wildfire. This burns all the trees and brush between the two fires. Because the original fire no longer has fuel in its path, it goes out.

Aerial ignition is one way to set a backfire. Small Ping-Pong-sized balls are shot from a helicopter. The balls explode after hitting the ground, releasing a chemical that sets the brush on fire.

Another more dangerous way of setting a backfire is to use a drip torch. A helicopter carries a fifty-five-gallon tank suspended on a long cable. The tank is filled with a mix of diesel fuel and gasoline. The mixture is ignited, and it will drip fire from a small spout onto the trees below.

≡ Dropping Fire Retardant

The huge tanks inside some air tankers can hold up to three thousand gallons of water or gooey liquid fire retardant. The retardant, which looks like a thick red soup, is a mixture of water, chemicals, and thickeners. It is so sticky that it clings to everything it touches. The chemicals soak the unburned plants and trees. This slows down fire and prevents it from spreading. Unlike water, the retardant does not evaporate in the intense heat. It is bright red so that the pilots can see where it lands. This way the next pilot will cover different ground with the next drop. The retardant contains fertilizer; it will seep into the soil and help new trees grow.

Some air tankers drop a foam retardant. To make foam, the pilot activates an onboard computerized chemical

This helicopter is starting a backfire using a drip torch. A tank filled with diesel fuel and gasoline hangs beneath the helicopter.

measurement system on the way to the fire. The computer controls a release of chemicals into the water. Mixing the chemicals with water makes the foam.

Foam retardant makes it easier to put out a fire. Foam bubbles hold the water on leaves, trees, and grass. The foam also slows down the evaporation of the water. Foam works better than water on the sides of hills and mountains because water naturally flows downhill and does not always stay where it is needed. Foam sticks to the bushes and low-growing plants and seeps into the ground. Coating an area with foam will usually stop a fire from spreading.

The height from which retardant is dropped is important. The pilots want to cover a section of 50 to 80 feet wide by 350 to 440 feet long.[3] The average drop altitude is about 150 to 200 feet above the treetops. If the drop begins too high, the wind will spread the retardant out away from the fire. The contents of an 800-gallon tank of retardant weigh 7,200 pounds.[4] If the retardant is dropped from too low, it can overturn fire trucks, crush trees, and kill anyone it hits.

Air tanker pilots fly into the wind when they drop foam or retardant chemicals on a fire. This slows the retardant quickly as it falls through the air. If it is done right, the retardant falls almost straight down, just in front of the fire.

CHAPTER 4

Smoke Jumper Training

Wildfires are often difficult and sometimes impossible to reach by roads. It may take two days to reach some fires using ground transportation.[1] When it is impossible to reach the fire from the road, smoke jumpers parachute from airplanes into the fire area. Smoke jumpers are often the first on the scene of a wildfire. They can go where even helicopters cannot land. They can usually reach a fire within an hour.

Smoke jumpers first began to fight fires in 1939. Their main job is to build fire lines, or firebreaks, around the fire. They cut down and remove all plants and trees in front of the fire. Their goal is to rob the fire of fuel.

A smoke jumper's work is hard and dangerous. They are trained to reach the wildfire and keep it from spreading. But they are also trained to stay alive. Just before the fire season begins, people of all different professions and backgrounds, including schoolteachers, lawyers, and students, head to smoke jumper training camps.

Before anyone tries out to become a smoke jumper, he or she spends at least three years as a hotshot, or ground firefighter. To qualify for smoke jumper school, a person has to do forty-five sit-ups, twenty-five push-ups, seven pull-ups, and a one-and-a-half-mile run—all in eleven minutes.[2] If the candidate can pass this test, he or she will begin four to six weeks of tough training.

In addition, each trainee must pass a pack-out test and a pack test during the first week of training. The pack-out test consists of carrying a 110-pound pack of smoke jumper equipment over a flat three-mile course in ninety minutes or less. The pack test requires carrying forty-five pounds over a flat three-mile course in forty-five minutes or less.[3]

One smoke jumper training camp is in the mountains of McCall, Idaho. The training is like a military boot camp. Some training days are fourteen to sixteen hours long. Students learn how to climb fifty-foot trees and how to use harnesses, belts, and three-inch spikes called gaffs on their boots. They use gaffs to dig into the tree to help them climb it. They learn how to dig fire lines and hike rugged trails while carrying eighty-pound packs. The

Smoke jumpers have parachutes with special handles that help steer them away from the fire as they drop into the danger zone.

smoke jumper trainees do push-ups every day, and they climb walls and ropes. They make practice parachute jumps from a 250-foot jump tower. They also make fifteen real parachute jumps from an airplane before they qualify as smoke jumpers.[4] They spend time in a classroom learning about fire-fighting and rescue methods.

The training is so tough that about 30 percent of the trainees quit.[5] Those who finish are able to walk 15 miles with 110-pound packs stuffed with their main parachute, reserve chute, personal gear, food, water, and tools.[6]

During this training, trainees spend several nights in the woods as if they were battling a real fire. They learn how to read maps and use the GPS. They help each other during the training because they know that on the fire line they will depend on each other for their lives.

Even though a smoke jumper can steer his parachute, sometimes one will get caught in a tall tree. To escape, the jumper ties and drops a rope from his pack and uses it to slide down to the ground. Trainees prepare for this situation by doing "let-downs"—rappelling practiced from a platform.

Protective Clothing

Smoke jumpers must wear protective clothing to guard themselves from the fire, trees, and any other obstacles they may hit as they descend to the ground. Their outer clothing is a jumpsuit made of two fabrics: Nomex and Kevlar. Nomex can resist fire, and Kevlar is the material used to make bulletproof vests. If the smoke jumper lands

All smoke jumpers carefully check each other's protective clothing. If their equipment is not on properly, they could be seriously injured or killed during the jump.

in the trees, the Kevlar will keep the tree branches from stabbing him. Smoke jumpers also wear a helmet with a wire face cage. The helmet protects their head, and the face cage protects their eyes and face from tree branches. A large high collar on their jumpsuit protects their neck.

Underneath the jumpsuit, smoke jumpers wear lightweight clothing. They work hard digging fire lines and climbing mountains. Heavy clothing would trap body heat. This, combined with the heat from the fire, would cause a smoke jumper's body temperature to rise to dangerous levels. When a person's body temperature gets too high, he or she can die.

When the alarm bell sounds at the Aerial Fire Depot in Missoula, Montana, the smoke jumpers quickly put on their protective clothing. They prepare to jump a fire.

CHAPTER 5

Taming the Flames

Awildfire is burning fifty miles from the Aerial Fire Depot in Missoula, Montana. The alarm bell sends the pilot running to his airplane.[1] Everything was ready even before the alarm bell had sounded. The airplane, a Basler BT-67, had had its external preflight checklist completed hours earlier. This is a visual inspection of the airplane. Among the many things the pilot looks for are cracks or other damage on the airplane. He or she also checks the tires to make sure they have enough air.

The twin-engine Basler BT-67 is a former Douglas DC-3 that was built in the late 1930s. It had served as an airliner and then as a cargo plane during World War II. After the

Specifications for
Basler BT-67

Wingspan—32 feet 8 inches
Height—23 feet 6 inches
Length—67 feet 9 inches
Wingspan—95 feet 8 inches
Engines—2
Crew—pilot, jump master, and 16 smoke jumpers
Cruise speed—236 miles per hour
Ceiling—20,000 feet
Tank capacity—1,000 gallons

war it carried passengers and freight. Now it will transport sixteen smoke jumpers to the wildfire.

Pilot Tom Bohannan climbs aboard the waiting airplane. He settles into the cockpit and begins his internal preflight checklist. This checklist is necessary to make sure all switches and levers are set in the right positions.

After completing the checklist, he starts the first engine. It begins to whine as the propeller begins to slowly turn. A muffled explosion of noise and a puff of white smoke follow a cough from the engine. The first of the airplane's two propellers are turning in a silver blur.

The BT-67 looks and feels like a brand-new airplane, because it practically is. It has many new parts, including two new turboprop engines. These powerful engines can pull it along at about 236 miles per hour. Each engine produces 1,281 horsepower. The plane can fly more than 20,000 feet high. For smoke-jumping missions, it usually does not fly higher than 1,500 feet above the ground.

By the time the engines are up to speed, sixteen smoke jumpers are on board. Bohannan taxis out to the runway and gets immediate clearance for takeoff. He pushes the two throttles forward. The airplane roars down the runway, picking up speed. Within seconds, it is airborne. Bohannan tips the big white bird to the left in a steep turn. He aims the airplane at a giant column of smoke in the distance.[2]

Fifteen minutes later, Bohannan and Walt Smith, the jump master, agree that a rocky hillside is the only drop zone clear of trees and close enough to the fire. The jump master is an important person on the airplane. He tells the jumpers when to jump. He drops two weighted crepe-paper streamers out the door of the airplane. The way the streamers fall indicates whether there are any strong winds. These winds can be dangerous for the jumpers.

The Basler BT-67 can transport up to sixteen smoke jumpers to the drop zone.

The wind could push the smoke jumpers over the fire. They do not want to drop into the fire, just close to it.

The pilot makes a second pass over the drop zone, and Smith drops a second set of streamers. If the timing is right, the second set of streamers will glide right into the proposed drop zone.

The Jump

The pilot begins to fly a long circular course, as if on a racetrack. At the drop point, the first two smoke jumpers will jump from the airplane.

Margarita Phillips is standing in the open doorway of the airplane. She is a smoke jumper, one of about four hundred in the United States. About twenty-five of them are women.[3] On this flight, she is the only woman. She is thirty-five years old and has five years of experience as a smoke jumper. Phillips calls upon all her training for this mission.[4]

Her eyes scan the drop zone 1,500 feet below. Her chin is tucked in and her face is hidden behind the wire cage on her helmet. The jump master is kneeling in the doorway. He taps her left leg. She pushes herself out the door. Seconds later, a second smoke jumper follows her into the sky. The plane continues to circle the drop zone. Fourteen more smoke jumpers follow Phillips, two at a time.

Above her, Phillips hears a pop. An instant later, she feels a sharp jerk on her shoulders. Her parachute has opened.

Phillips falls toward the blazing landscape below. Her parachute is her main piece of equipment. It has about eight hundred square feet of nylon and hundreds of yards of line. It slows her fall to about fifteen miles per hour. The ride down lasts about seventy-five seconds, and Phillips will hit the ground very hard. Sometimes the wind tries to push her toward the fire. Phillips uses the control-line toggles on her parachute to steer herself to a safe landing near, but not in, the fire.

Every jump Phillips makes is dangerous. The temperature of the fire below her is about 2,600 degrees Fahrenheit. It is hot enough to melt steel. She steers her parachute away from heat that could disintegrate her

As the smoke jumper leaves the airplane, the static cord will automatically begin to open the parachute.

eyelashes. Her skin would blister in seconds if she got too close to the fire.

When all the smoke jumpers are on the ground, the airplane flies back over them. The jump master drops most of the tools and equipment by parachute. This is most of the equipment the smoke jumpers will need to fight the wildfire, including chain saws and gasoline, rakes, Pulaskis (combination ax and hoe), freeze-dried food, instant cereal, drinking water, and sleeping bags.

Once on the ground, Phillips and the other smoke jumpers collect all the equipment. Then they begin to fight the wildfire. There is usually no water nearby to use to fight the fire, so they cut down anything that can burn—trees, bushes, and shrubs—from in front of the fire. They pull out all the grass and gather the leaves that can burn. They also use chain saws to cut down big trees in the fire's path. Cutting down the trees will stop the fire from leaping from tree to tree and spreading even farther. The smoke jumpers may also light backfires to burn the wildfire out.

After the fire is out, the smoke jumpers' work is still not over. They will spend days digging through the burned-out area with their Pulaskis. This tool can chop through branches and bushes. The smoke jumpers turn the dirt and ash over, looking for smoldering embers that could start the fire all over again.

To make sure the fire is out, the smoke jumpers crawl on their hands and knees, doing what they call grubbing potatoes. They take off their gloves and pat the ground,

Most of the supplies the smoke jumpers need are dropped by parachute after they have landed safely on the ground.

feeling for warm earth. They probe with their fingers to make sure all the hot spots are out. After every smoldering ember is extinguished, the firefighters hike down the mountain, where a helicopter airlifts them back to their base.

Backyard Fires

Not all wildfires occur in remote mountain regions. Some come roaring into people's backyards. Usually ground firefighters fight these fires, but for large, out-of-control fires, air tankers and helicopters are called in.

On November 2, 1993, a brush fire started in Old Topanga Canyon, in the Santa Monica Mountains of California. The canyon acted like a chimney, with a draft that sucked the flames upward. The Santa Anas, strong winds that blow over Southern California every year, fanned the flames. The forty-mile-per-hour winds pushed the flames so fast that in ten minutes, two hundred acres were on fire. The heat from the fire dried out everything in front of it, and trees were bursting into flames. Many homes in Old Topanga Canyon were in the path of the fire, and the lives of hundreds of people were in danger.

Helicopters started dropping 3,000-gallon buckets of water on the fire. They flew to the Pacific Ocean, filled their Bambi Buckets, and dumped the water on the flames. The fire raged for ten days and nights, while the helicopters and air tankers kept making their drops. County of Los Angeles Fire Department helicopters made 750 drops, and the U.S. Forest Service dropped more than one million gallons of fire retardant. When the fire was finally out, more than 16,500 acres of woodlands and whole neighborhoods had disappeared. All that marked the spot where 388 homes had stood were charred brick chimneys. Three people died, and hundreds of firefighters and twenty-one civilians were injured.[5]

The individuals who fly fire-fighting aircraft are highly trained and motivated. They fly through smoke and over red-hot cinders to drop fire retardant to stop fires from spreading. Fixed-wing and helicopter tankers drop water and foam on fires to put them out. When air strikes do not succeed in putting the fires out, smoke jumpers parachute into the danger zone to fight the fires. The pilots and smoke jumpers put themselves at great personal risk to extinguish fires, while saving property, wildlife, and, most importantly, people's lives.

Chapter Notes

Chapter 1. Wildfire

1. Edwin Kiester, Jr., "Battling the Orange Monster," *Smithsonian*, July 2000, p. 37.

2. Ibid.

3. Ibid.

Chapter 2. Flying on the Edge of Danger

1. Author correspondence with Jean Bergerson, Information Officer, Fire Control Center, Grand Rapids, Michigan, April 13, 2001.

2. Associated Press, "Air Tankers Collide Fighting Fires; Two Pilots Killed," *FOXNews.com*, August 28, 2001, <http://www.foxnews.com/story/0,2933,33042,00.html> (August 28, 2001).

3. Barry D. Smith, *Fire Bombers in Action* (Osceola, Wis.: Motorbooks International, 1995), p. 52.

4. California Department of Forestry and Fire Protection, "Short Haul Rescue," n.d., <www.fire.ca.gov/FireEmergencyResponse/Aviation/PDF/shorthaul.pdf> (February 13, 2002).

5. Valerie Alvord, "Firefighters Take Work to New Heights. It's Hot, Dangerous Work as Pilots Attack Blazes from the Sky," *USA Today*, August 7, 2000, p. A3.

6. Edwin Kiester, Jr., "Battling the Orange Monster," *Smithsonian*, July 2000, p. 32.

7. Smith, p. 34.

Chapter 3. Fire-Fighting Equipment

1. Goddard Space Flight Center, "NASA Satellite, University of Maryland and U.S. Forest Service Provide Rapid Response to Wildfires," August 20, 2001, <http://www.gsfc.nasa.gov/news-release/releases/2001/01-83.htm> (February 13, 2002).

2. Paul Proctor, "Fire-Fighting Fleet Stretched to Limits as U.S. West Burns," *Aviation Week & Space Technology*, August 21, 2000, p. 38.

3. Matthew L. Wald, "Florida's Flatland and Shrubs a Haven for Fires," *The New York Times*, July 8, 1998, p. 16.

4. Barry D. Smith, *Fire Bombers in Action* (Osceola, Wis.: Motorbooks International, 1995), p. 28.

Chapter 4. Smoke Jumper Training

1. Tom Harpole, "The Smokejumpers," *Air & Space*, August/September 1993, p. 34.

2. USDA Forest Service, "McCall Smokejumpers," n.d., <http://www.fs.fed.us/fire/operations/jumpers/mccall/> (February 13, 2002).

3. Ibid.

4. Ibid.

5. Jo-Ann Johnston, "Into the Fire," *Tampa Tribune*, November 30, 2000, Baylife Section, p. 6.

6. Harpole, p. 35.

Chapter 5. Taming the Flames

1. Discovery Communication, Inc., "Line of Fire: New Respect for an Old Enemy," *Discovery.com*, © 2001, <www.discovery.com/area/science/wildfires/wildfires.html> (September 1, 2001).

2. Ibid.

3. Jo-Ann Johnston, "Into the Fire," *Tampa Tribune*, November 30, 2000, Baylife Section, p. 1.

4. Discovery Communication, Inc.

5. County of Los Angeles Fire Department, Official Report, Old Topanga Incident, November 2, 1993 to November 11, 1993, <www.lafire.com/famous_fires/ 931102_OldTopangaFire/110293_official_report_old_ topanga_inci.htm> (December 1, 2001).

Glossary

air strike—A combination of aerial tankers and helicopters that drop fire retardant, foam, or water on a fire.

air tanker—Large propeller-driven airplane that drops water and retardant chemicals over a fire.

backfire—A fire set in front of a wildfire designed to limit the spread of the wildfire.

Bambi Bucket—A bucket suspended from a helicopter that can be filled with water and dumped over a fire.

drip torch—A device that drips ignited fuel oil and gasoline from a helicopter to start a backfire.

fire line (firebreak)—A path along which all flammable materials such as brush, fallen trees, and roots are removed.

fire retardant—Chemicals that slow down the spread of a wildfire.

FLIR—Forward-looking infrared sensor. FLIR detects the heat from an aircraft, a fire, an animal, or people and displays it on a monitor similar to a television screen.

gaff—A spike on a smoke jumper's boot used to help him or her climb trees.

GPS—Global Positioning System. A network of U.S. satellites that transmits radio signals for navigation.

helitack—A mission that involves helicopters carrying giant buckets of water.

hotshot—A ground firefighter.

hover—To stay in the air without moving in any direction.

lead plane—The aircraft that determines the size and direction of a fire and leads air tankers over a fire.

preflight checklist—A visual inspection of an aircraft before takeoff.

rappelling—To descend by sliding down a rope.

smoke jumpers—Firefighters who parachute from airplanes to fight wildfires.

Further Reading

Books

Beil, Karen Magnuson. *Fire in Their Eyes: Wildfires and the People Who Fight Them*. New York: Harcourt Brace & Company, 1999.

Greenberg, Keith. *Firefighter from the Sky*. San Diego, Calif.: Blackbirch Press, Incorporated, 1995.

Hines, Gary. *Flying Firefighters*. New York: Houghton Mifflin Company, 1993.

Holden, Henry M. *Black Hawk Helicopter*. Berkeley Heights, N.J.: Enslow Publishers, Inc., 2001.

Vogt, Gregory. *Forests on Fire: The Fight to Save Our Trees*. New York: Franklin Watts Incorporated, 1990.

Internet Addresses

California Department of Forestry and Fire Protection. *Welcome to CDF*. n.d. <http://www.fire.ca.gov/>

Smokejumpers.com. *National Smokejumpers Association*. © 2001. <http://www.smokejumpers.com/>

USDA Forest Service and the National Association of State Foresters. *Smokey Bear: Only you can prevent wildfires!* © 1998. <http://www.smokeybear.com/>